Become a Chief Couponing Officer!

A Money Saving Guide and Math Workbook

By: Sorina Fant

Sorina Fant

www.SorinaFant.com

Chief Couponing Officer

Table of Contents

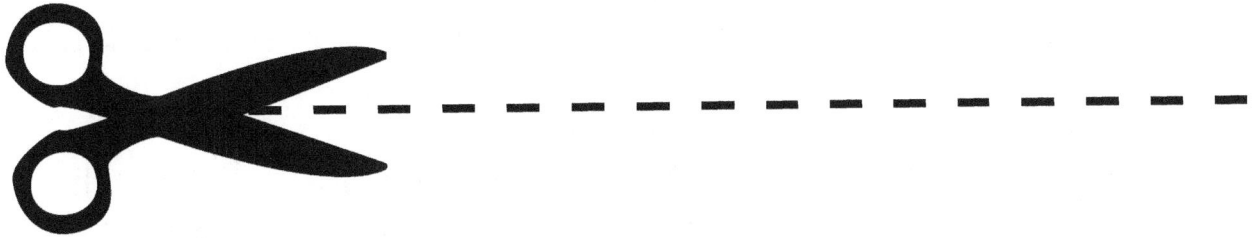

1. The Original Chief Couponing Officer- CCO - page 4

2. Couponing Tips! - pages 5-7

3. Tips for Hosting a Family Meeting - page 8

4. Dinner Menu Template - page 9

5. Grocery List Template - pages 10-11

6. Adding and Subtracting Money - pages 12-27

7. Fractions and the Importance of DIY - pages 28-33

8. In Store Savings -pages 34-39

9. Multiplication - pages 40-51

10. Take a Trial Run! - pages 52-56

11. Divide Your Savings by 3 - pages 57-60

12. Savings Log - pages 61-71

13. How Much Did You Save This Year? - page 72

14. What's Next? Become a Personal Shopper - page 73

The Original Chief Couponing Officer

When I was younger, I struggled with math. I was a good student and excelled in most subjects, but I was not super confident when it came to math. When my math grades started to slip in school, my mother, a couponer, passed the torch to me. She allowed me to earn an allowance by creating a dinner menu, a grocery list and clipping the coupons for the weekly grocery shopping trip. On average I was able to save $60 per week on our grocery bill and I earned a percentage of the total savings as a reward for my hardwork. I loved my role as my family's Chief Couponing Officer and enjoyed having extra money to spend as well as money to save for a rainy day.

I was my family's Chief Couponing Officer - a title that I was extremely proud to have. Over time, my couponing skills became stronger and my math grades started to increase. I had confidence in the classroom as well as the grocery store. My family saved money on groceries, I had more money in my savings account and I was back on the honor roll. Win, win, win!

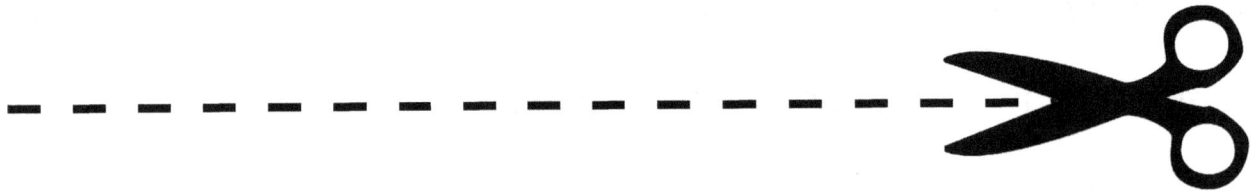

And now that I am an adult, I want to share my journey of becoming a Chief Couponing Officer with others. My hope is that all families will understand the value of using coupons. So many coupons go unused each week - this is literally free savings that go right in the trash! All families, no matter their budget, can benefit from saving money on groceries. Everyone will appreciate extra money saved with couponing!

Plus, whether you are a student who already loves math or whether you are more like me and need an extra boost to find your confidence in the subject, couponing is your answer! Couponing makes a math fan out of everyone and will also help to establish great financial habits that will last a lifetime.

Couponing Tips!

Before you jump into your role as a Chief Couponing Officer, keep the following tips in mind...

1. Stay Organized!

Even before you actually start cutting and collecting your coupons, you need to have a system to keep everything organized. Invest in a storage box, binder clips, a medium sized accordion envelope, a small calculator and a few pens and pencils. For a complete couponing kit including everything that you need, visit www.sorinafant.com under "Couponing Supplies."

2. Start a coupon stockpile!

It is important to make sure that you utilize several different resources in order to collect all the coupons that you need. Don't be afraid to ask family members, friends, neighbors, even your principal and teacher for coupons that they are not using. So many people have coupons that they end up throwing away but a Chief Couponing Officer knows how to put them to good use! Suggest to your parents, if you don't already do, to subscribe to the your local paper. You don't need to get the paper every day, but the Sunday morning edition will give you hundreds of dollars in savings every week. Plus the Sunday paper contains sales papers to your local grocery store, which is key to finding the best deals when shopping. If subscribing to your local paper is not an option, plan to pick up the sales paper at the grocery store prior to your shopping trip.

3. Print coupons from the Internet and write letters to specific companies.

With your parent's permission, visit sites from the some of your favorite products and print coupons for specific products that your family uses. Plus if you send emails to companies and tell them about the items that you use, they will usually send you additional coupons, as they like to keep loyal customers happy and purchasing additional products.

More Couponing Tips...

4. Small savings are still a BIG deal!

Don't worry about saving a ton of money on coupons right away. It takes awhile to get into a rhythm with couponing. Over time you will become an expert Chief Couponing Officer and know how to handle the juggle of sales papers, family meetings and finding the best deals. Don't be afraid to start small. Clip coupons for toilet paper, laundry detergent and dishwashing soap. Search the sales papers to find out when those products are on sale. Try to take advantage of those deals. Once you save a few dollars on your first couponing trip, you will be hooked and will want to keep going!

5. Do your homework!

It is incredibly important to know the couponing policy for your local grocery store. Some stores allow for double coupons on specific days while some don't have double coupons at all. Plus your local store may restrict the number of coupons that you can use, which can limit the number of products that you purchase at one time - especially if you are adding to your stockpile. Make sure to do your homework and know all of the rules prior to shopping.

6. Know what you have!

Take inventory every week of the products that you already have at home. Check the pantry and the freezer before each trip to the grocery store. So many households waste hundreds of dollars every year when they throw away products that expire before they are consumed or continue to buy items again and again when they don't need to. A true Chief Couponing Officer knows when to save and when to spend!

7. Take advantage of in-store savings

While the goal is to save your family as much money as possible while grocery shopping, it is important to always think ahead. There are certain products that you will always need (toothpaste, toilet paper, etc.) and while they may not be needed that particular week, it is wise to make sure that you take advantage of in-store sales when they are available. Unless you are on a weekly budget, don't pass up an amazing deal when you can.

8. Have fun!

There is nothing more exciting than seeing how much money you can save on your grocery bill. So relax, stay organized and enjoy being a Chief Couponing Officer!

Tips for Hosting a Family Meeting

A good Chief Couponing Officer is a leader that strives to not only save their family the most money on groceries, but they make sure that everyone in the family is excited about the healthy menu for the week. Keep the following tips in mind when calling a family meeting:

1. Be Prepared. Bring a blank copy of the dinner menu, the shopping list and a pen.

2. Read the sales paper aloud. When trying to save as much as you can on the weekly meals, it is always best to check out the front page of the sales papers. The front page is the perfect spot to find the products that have been marked down the most. For example, if packs of ground turkey are half-off, suggest a taco night or spaghetti with ground turkey meatballs. Creating meals off of the sales paper will allow you to be creative with family meals and save a ton of money on each dinner. Plus the sales papers will always advertise the seasonal vegetables that are on sale, which means your family will have an inexpensive, nutritious meal.

3. Give everyone a chance to contribute ideas including suggestions for lunch and breakfast. The more everyone's opinions are shared, the greater the chances are that family dinners will be enjoyed.

4. Before ending the meeting, make sure to ask everyone if there are any personal items that they need (deodorant, shampoo, body wash, etc.). Add these items to the shopping list.

5. Once the meeting is over, finish the shopping list. Go through the refrigerator and pantry to see what items you have and what other items that you need for all of the meals for the week.

DINNER MENU

Monday: _____

Tuesday: _____

Wednesday: _____

Thursday: _____

Friday: _____

Saturday: _____

Sunday: _____

GROCERY LIST

Produce:

_____   _____

_____   _____

_____   _____

_____   _____

_____   _____

Meat and Dairy:

_____   _____

_____   _____

_____   _____

Cereal/Grains/Snacks:

_____   _____

_____   _____

Cleaning Products/Laundry Products:

_____   _____

_____   _____

_____   _____

GROCERY LIST

Baking and Cooking Items:

_____   _____

_____   _____

Canned Products:

_____   _____

_____   _____

Beauty and Health Products:

_____   _____

_____   _____

_____   _____

Baked Goods:

_____   _____

_____   _____

Other Items:

_____   _____

_____   _____

_____   _____

_____   _____

_____   _____

_____   _____

Adding and Subtracting Money

When it comes to adding and subtracting money, the most important thing to remember is to ALWAYS LINE UP YOUR DECIMALS. If you don't line up your decimals, your calculations will never be correct. The best way to add or subtract money is to make your problem vertical, line up your decimals and calculate the sum or the difference.

The right way! :)

$$\begin{array}{r} \$34.20 \\ +\ \ 1.92 \\ \hline \end{array}$$

$$\begin{array}{r} \$34.20 \\ +1.92 \\ \hline \end{array}$$

The wrong way! :(

Let's try a few samples...

Solve the following problems. Make sure to use the extra space to turn the problem vertical. Don't forget to double check your work and add the dollar sign to your answer.

sample) $55.11+$22.30 =

sample) $16.00-$2.33 =

Adding Money

Answer the following addition problems.

1) $80.81
   +45.60

2) $49.11
   +43.43

3) $86.55
   +52.97

4) $61.43
   +31.63

5) $32.54
   +20.78

6) $76.99
   +12.32

7) $27.91
   +25.33

8) $55.92
   +48.12

9) $63.63
   +19.16

10) $77.77
    +12.52

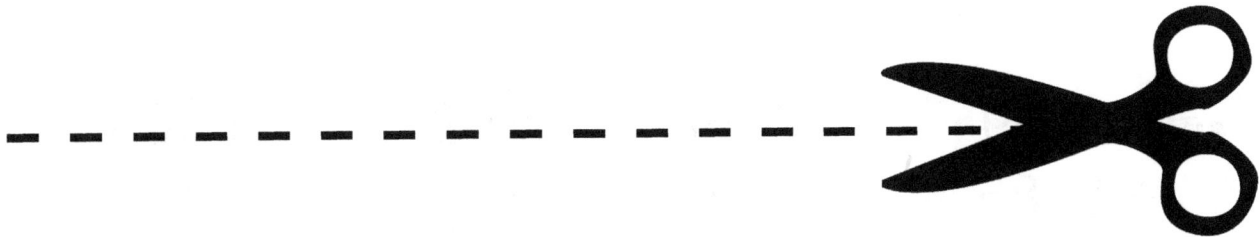

11) $59.11
    +44.70

12) $32.33
    +14.17

13) $64.50
    +23.88

14) $20.30
    +15.43

15) $29.67
    +13.40

16) $55.27
    +17.48

17) $92.90
    + 2.99

18) $41.99
    +39.55

19) $84.84
    +69.22

20) $87.81
    +16.98

21) $66.70
    +38.42

22) $49.46
    +29.22

More Addition...

Keep going! Make sure to double check your work and add dollar signs and decimals to your answers.

23) $42.22
+37.55

24) $63.67
+44.96

25) $91.11
+54.53

26) $71.35
+62.90

27) $92.50
+14.77

28) $26.86
+26.70

29) $51.90
+19.60

30) $53.77
+27.88

31) $28.99
+25.85

32) $43.66
+26.81

33) $59.81
+29.80

34) $63.91
+34.61

35) $20.77
+19.45

36) $66.55
+30.51

37) $64.01
+51.99

38) $45.45
+37.22

39) $81.82
+35.87

40) $32.78
+27.35

41) $52.99
+87.11

42) $73.33
+48.15

43) $86.77
+53.09

44) $22.41
+20.99

45) $72.88
+66.99

46) $87.22
+72.98

47) $63.30
   +17.88

48) $24.77
   +17.39

49) $29.28
   +13.99

50) $61.69
   +60.77

51) $91.28
   +79.11

52) $86.22
   +19.97

53) $77.60
   +10.09

54) $81.18
   +80.17

55) $19.99
   +18.88

56) $33.33
   +29.95

57) $59.55
   +41.32

58) $70.81
   +51.99

59) $39.93
   +28.77

60) $78.76
   +69.96

61) $88.99
   +71.17

62) $59.86
   +49.93

63) $76.69
   +45.33

64) $41.88
   +37.99

65) $71.19
   +29.87

66) $52.27
   +38.16

67) $66.95
   +41.15

68) $95.08
   +11.61

69) $77.81
   +66.11

70) $55.47
   +33.96

Adding Hundreds

71) $542.17
  + 416.38

72) $277.89
  + 199.54

73) $611.99
  + 226.77

74) $326.88
  + 299.67

75) $380.93
  + 188.95

76) $633.88
  + 622.09

77) $887.93
  + 644.49

78) $808.88
  + 545.22

79) $677.77
  + 509.88

80) $399.99
  + 286.62

81) $711.93
  + 707.88

82) $922.55
  + 654.31

83) $445.80
  + 377.95

84) $688.20
  + 555.99

85) $377.43
  + 288.93

86) $755.80
  + 611.94

87) $288.88
  + 190.65

88) $554.99
  + 412.88

89) $397.77
  + 336.88

90) $767.73
  + 688.88

91) $771.44
  + 770.55

More Adding...

92) $397.77
+ 336.88

93) $709.22
+ 611.99

94) $554.92
+ 339.99

95) $322.44
+ 321.88

96) $997.33
+ 798.44

97) $888.93
+ 711.17

98) $542.18
+ 539.99

99) $522.29
+ 477.89

100) $452.19
+ 229.95

101) $770.98
+ 472.22

102) $866.32
+ 722.07

103) $566.78
+ 308.06

104) $803.55
+ 299.89

105) $911.18
+ 880.48

106) $229.93
+ 188.88

107) $707.77
+ 291.10

108) $333.37
+ 218.88

109) $899.92
+ 887.77

Adding Thousands

110) $1668.22
+ 1334.58

111) $3352.53
+ 1888.32

112) $7773.51
+ 6880.23

113) $4221.77
+ 3299.60

114) $5566.72
+ 5111.99

115) $9898.33
+ 6144.62

116) $8002.66
+ 7144.29

117) $2886.33
+ 2009.99

118) $4900.88
+ 4888.97

119) $3998.70
+ 3009.11

120) $7676.99
+ 4900.04

121) $6694.44
+ 5551.15

122) $5332.71
+ 1990.98

123) $9002.34
+ 8777.54

124) $8877.33
+ 7866.39

125) $4311.19
+ 3773.79

126) $6625.50
+ 6577.99

127) $9880.43
+ 3347.80

128) $4110.43
+ 4008.08

129) $7743.99
+ 6112.25

130) $7911.16
+ 3211.68

Subtracting Money

1) $23.67
- 17.88

2) $34.43
- 31.99

3) $76.09
- 64.44

4) $53.56
- 50.08

5) $89.07
- 87.11

6) $60.78
- 56.99

7) $62.21
- 55.89

8) $44.33
- 28.01

9) $22.24
- 19.99

10) $47.72
- 39.55

11) $17.80
- 14.12

12) $55.65
- 29.74

13) $66.23
- 50.50

14) $28.87
- 16.90

15) $69.45
- 61.22

16) $33.32
- 21.88

17) $43.42
- 35.80

18) $90.22
- 87.44

19) $57.79
- 46.12

20) $89.12
- 67.00

21) $66.12
- 39.82

22) $88.02
- 19.56

23) $66.88
- 59.99

24) $31.31
- 22.78

25) $19.30
- 11.99

26) $50.04
- 29.66

27) $47.20
- 28.87

28) $83.30
- 55.95

More Subtraction...

29) $19.30
   - 11.99
   _____

30) $55.32
   - 45.88
   _____

31) $70.14
   - 65.53
   _____

32) $90.11
   - 64.20
   _____

33) $23.89
   - 18.88
   _____

34) $84.20
   - 31.15
   _____

35) $61.21
   - 44.90
   _____

36) $72.78
   - 30.08
   _____

37) $23.66
   - 19.70
   _____

38) $58.02
   - 30.97
   _____

39) $32.32
   - 28.70
   _____

40) $88.94
   - 76.64
   _____

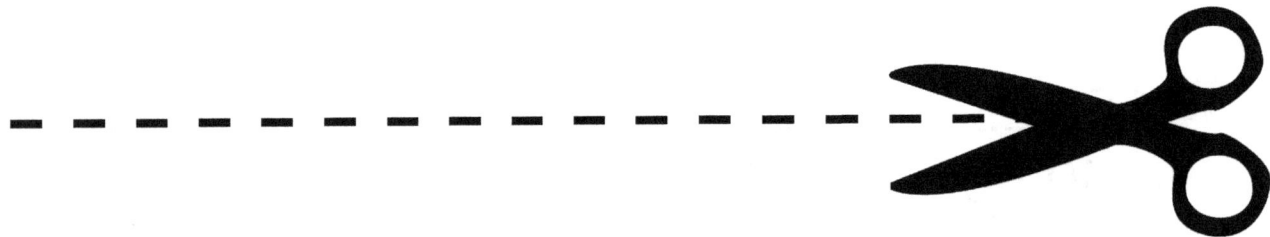

41) $50.97
   - 42.31
   _____

42) $30.01
   - 23.66
   _____

43) $57.70
   - 30.30
   _____

44) $97.22
   - 55.50
   _____

45) $73.00
   - 16.99
   _____

46) $80.28
   - 66.30
   _____

47) $28.31
   - 20.88
   _____

48) $90.90
   - 64.52
   _____

49) $79.56
   - 52.18
   _____

50) $68.04
   - 41.11
   _____

51) $80.20
   - 33.99
   _____

52) $59.99
   - 43.07
   _____

Subtracting Hundreds

53) $445.12
 - 377.60

54) $636.33
 - 289.09

55) $717.69
 - 505.14

56) $511.90
 - 488.04

57) $818.55
 - 421.87

58) $594.67
 - 144.55

59) $648.11
 - 500.70

60) $996.33
 - 887.19

61) $108.09
 - 89.12

62) $176.43
 - 121.29

63) $266.90
 - 111.17

64) $468.80
 - 317.23

65) $766.03
 - 599.25

66) $621.13
 - 444.99

67) $823.76
 - 500.49

68) $771.23
 - 505.15

69) $299.44
 - 267.12

70) $919.23
 - 141.16

71) $390.39
 - 222.62

72) $411.14
 - 166.80

73) $789.98
 - 671.19

More Subtracting Hundreds...

74) $265.56
- 199.99

75) $490.03
- 343.39

76) $882.81
- 330.92

77) $515.57
- 360.78

78) $507.79
- 400.95

79) $601.26
- 227.89

80) $886.45
- 453.80

81) $209.43
- 133.38

82) $779.02
- 219.99

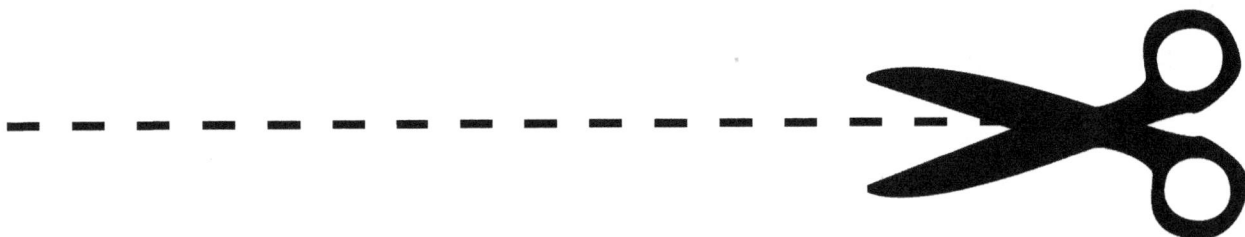

83) $334.45
- 197.50

84) $789.00
- 560.23

85) $500.60
- 421.33

86) $898.80
- 340.02

87) $383.35
- 299.45

88) $917.93
- 836.61

89) $733.31
- 699.39

90) $255.02
- 167.21

91) $557.78
- 321.19

Subtracting Thousands

92) $5177.80
- 3006.12

93) $8989.60
- 7610.09

94) $7119.22
- 5656.77

95) $4003.66
- 2990.38

96) $8009.32
- 6704.42

97) $2964.45
- 1903.22

98) $1416.34
- 1299.99

99) $6702.53
- 4955.55

100) $8680.84
- 5110.90

101) $1600.29
- 987.67

102) $8833.71
- 5699.29

103) $9920.65
- 6777.90

104) $5777.90
- 4499.29

105) $8002.67
- 5600.98

106) $2121.78
- 1999.43

107) $8118.22
- 6500.08

108) $6116.70
- 5900.15

109) $5967.10
- 3788.89

110) $4700.89
- 3211.90

111) $1199.80
- 1077.31

112) $6600.99
- 2307.77

Adding and Subtracting Money

Pay attention to the signs and circle all addition problems.

1) $711.68
  - 332.17

2) $545.55
  + 311.29

3) $661.19
  - 569.92

4) $229.10
  + 189.28

5) $557.89
  + 311.09

6) $850.02
  - 661.24

7) $992.94
  + 707.78

8) $555.78
  - 425.60

9) $662.16
  + 545.78

10) $311.16
  - 255.89

11) $222.75
  - 177.22

12) $440.02
  - 188.86

13) $665.11
  + 400.02

14) $888.12
  + 200.14

15) $622.31
  - 340.77

16) $990.87
  - 886.43

17) $897.70
  + 611.08

18) $577.78
  - 229.09

19) $330.15
  + 288.55

20) $400.45
  - 312.27

21) $990.24
  + 882.28

24

More Adding and Subtracting Money...

Pay attention to the signs and circle all subtraction problems.

22) $5122.33
   + 3434.90

23) $8802.12
   - 6543.31

24) $7111.01
   - 4559.03

25) $8444.55
   + 6900.06

26) $2212.12
   + 1777.30

27) $2323.67
   - 1988.80

28) $3398.17
   + 1155.76

29) $7070.23
   - 3111.18

30) $4127.34
   + 2999.21

31) $3677.21
   + 2119.97

32) $8678.88
   - 5300.99

33) $5789.12
   - 4097.73

34) $8155.60
   - 6888.21

35) $3434.70
   + 2883.37

36) $9077.00
   - 7074.39

37) $6780.02
   - 3877.18

38) $1998.60
   + 1007.79

39) $4422.18
   + 2909.85

More Adding and Subtracting Money...

Keep going! Pay attention to the signs. Put a heart next to all the addition problems.

40) $65,321.98
+ 15,788.11

41) $41,445.78
- 22,989.34

42) $31,313.42
+ 27,879.65

43) $98,932.43
- 11,410.08

44) $62,214.55
+ 61,763.38

45) $77,217.90
- 23,344.48

46) $29,993.25
- 27,311.88

47) $88,800.05
- 44,588.93

48) $56,567.22
+ 51,333.27

49) $64,615.88
+ 41,119.80

50) $29,814.46
- 26,114.80

51) $90,003.28
+ 80,129.99

52) $44,412.28
+ 19,888.21

53) $59,900.22
- 52,280.15

54) $72,244.61
- 64,122.27

55) $89,000.33
- 47,789.10

56) $13,288.90
+ 11,800.55

57) $39,999.21
+ 32,665.19

58) $61,177.34
 - 15,129.90

59) $81,222.65
 + 78,800.23

60) $90,992.18
 - 44,477.80

61) $41,677.78
 + 39,904.55

62) $77,791.12
 - 63,300.99

63) $26,677.12
 + 19,990.25

64) $36,660.09
 - 22,677.71

65) $55,518.89
 + 47,790.88

66) $33,312.90
 + 28,800.07

67) $98,112.17
 + 76,770.78

68) $38,880.55
 - 22,286.03

69) $19,199.32
 - 18,700.15

70) $66,789.04
 - 52,522.57

71) $41,114.46
 - 37,711.17

72) $80,004.55
 + 15,519.04

73) $92,922.92
 + 79,988.05

74) $28,144.48
 - 17,788.85

75) $45,002.23
 + 37,767.97

Fractions and the Importance of DIY

One of the major ways to cut down on your family's grocery bill is to not only use coupons but to find ways in which you can save money by becoming a DIY (or do-it-yourself) expert. You can make many products and food items at a FRACTION of the cost. A FRACTION is a piece or a part of a whole. For example, a slice of pizza is a FRACTION of the entire pie. A DIY product costs a FRACTION of the price of the original product because you made it yourself.

For instance, a bottle of concentrated floor cleaner that you would use to mop the floor with could cost you up to $5.25 for just one use! That price adds up and often you need to use the entire bottle to clean the floor. If you mop your floor once a week, that is an average cost of $21 per month and $126 every six months on floor cleaner alone! :(

However, you can make your own floor cleaner with vinegar (the gallon could cost $8), baking soda (a one pound box can cost $5) and a few tablespoons of dishwashing soap (a 24 ounce bottle can cost $2.50). While the DIY version of floor cleaner costs $15.50 prior to using coupons, those items will give you enough cleaner to wash your floors for up to six months!

Floor Cleaner Recipe
3 gallons of water
2 cups of vinegar
1 cup of baking soda
5 tablespoons of dishwashing detergent

This version of floor cleaner will cost your family less than $3 per month!

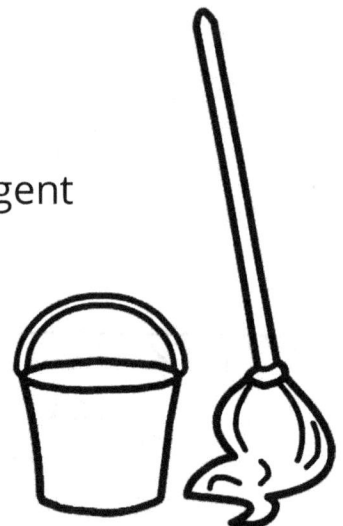

Once you finish moping the floor, why not make yourself a delicious treat? My frozen ice cream is a fraction of the cost of a half a gallon of ice cream and it's healthier for you.

Yummy Chocolate Chip Banana Ice Cream

Place frozen bananas, peanut butter and honey in a food processor. Once smooth, scoop into a large bowl. Mix in the chocolate chips. Serve and enjoy!

8 bananas (peeled and frozen)
5 tablespoons of peanut butter
3 tablespoons of honey
1/3 of a cup of chocolate chips

This healthier version of ice cream is 1/5 of the cost of the average half gallon of ice cream!

Baked Parmesan French Fries

Russet Potatoes (1 per person)
Olive oil
Sea Salt
Pepper
Grated Parmesan Cheese
1. Set oven to 350 degrees.
2. Clean, peel and cut potatoes into fries.
3. Rinse and soak fries in cold water for 10 minutes.
4. Spray a cookie sheet with a non-stick spray and spread fries where they do not overlap.
5. Sprinkle olive oil, parmesan cheese, sea salt and pepper over fries.
6. Bake for 15-20 minutes or or longer if you like crispy fries.

These parmesan fries are healthier, and cheaper than the pre-packaged french fries at only 1/3 of the cost.

More Fractions...

It is important to understand FRACTIONS when couponing. Many coupons will offer half-off (or 50%) of the purchase price and half-off is a FRACTION of the total price. Therefore, using a half-off coupon means that 50% of the total price of an item will be subtracted. For example, your favorite cereal is normally $5. You have a 50% off coupon meaning that $2.50 will be removed from the price. You will only pay the remaining half, which is $2.50.

Let's practice FRACTIONS! Try to figure out 1/2 off of the following amounts.

1) 1/2 of $100 = _____

2) 1/2 of $20 = _____

3) 1/2 of $1= _____

4) 1/2 of $12 = _____

5) 1/2 of $150 = _____

6) 1/2 of $2.50 = _____

7) 1/2 of $500 = _____

8) 1/2 of $700 = _____

9) 1/2 of $30 = _____

10) 1/2 of $44 = _____

11) 1/2 of $80 = _____

12) 1/2 of $0.50 = _____

13) 1/2 of $900 = _____

14) 1/2 of $550 = _____

15) 1/2 of $620 = _____

16) 1/2 of $830 = _____

17) 1/2 of $950 = _____

18) 1/2 of $406 = _____

19) 1/2 of $844 = _____

20) 1/2 of $610 = _____

21) 1/2 of $52 = _____

22) 1/2 of $88 = _____

23) 1/2 of $24 = _____

24) 1/2 of $92 = _____

25) 1/2 of $222 = _____

26) 1/2 of $330 = _____

27) 1/2 of $880 = _____

28) 1/2 of $710 = _____

29) 1/2 of $444 = _____

30) 1/2 of $18 = _____

31) 1/2 of $150 = _____

32) 1/2 of $230 = _____

33) 1/2 of $208 = _____

34) 1/2 of $404 = _____

35) 1/2 of $130 = _____

36) 1/2 of $360 = _____

37) 1/2 of $102 = _____

38) 1/2 of $912 = _____

39) 1/2 of $716 = _____

40) 1/2 of $440 = _____

More Fractions...

41) Bags of baby carrots are originally priced at $2.50 each. You have three 1/2 off coupons. You eat baby carrots in your lunch every day so this is a great deal! What is the total cost for all three bags after the coupons savings?

42) Your family needs more mouthwash and your usual brand is normally $8.50. You have a 1/2 off coupon that expires today so you need to use it immediately. How much does the bottle of mouthwash cost?

43) Your little brother loves peanut butter and honey sandwiches for lunch. Because he eats them every day, you need to purchase at least one jar of peanut butter for the week. One jar of organic peanut butter costs $3.60. What is the cost of the jar of peanut butter after using your 1/2 off coupon?

44) One roll of aluminum foil costs $1.25. However, they have a pack of 3 rolls that cost $3.30 (which is a savings of $0.45) and you have a coupon for half-off. How much will the 3 pack cost after applying your 1/2 off coupon?

45) Your mother wants to make her famous hummus. She needs two bags of dried garbanzo beans. Each bag costs $1.30. You have a half-off coupon for only one of the bags. What is the total price for both bags?

46) Your family is attending a potluck at your school on Saturday night and your father volunteered to bring his delicious spaghetti. He needs 3 large cans of tomato sauce for his marinara. Each can costs $2.22. You have 2 coupons for 1/2 off two of the cans. What is the total cost for the 3 cans of tomato sauce?

In Store Savings

It is incredibly important to always be on the lookout for in-store savings. They are often not advertised in the sales papers but if you take advantage of them, they can be huge money savers for your family. Often this calls for you to be more aware of the products that you are putting in your basket, as there may be a coupon that is stuck to the side of an item you are purchasing. You may even need to purchase an item or two that is not on your list to take advantage of savings. However, if the potential savings are worth it, go for it! Saving on your weekly grocery bill is great but savings over a long-term period is EXCELLENT!

Let's try a few in-store scenerios...

1) Every Friday is family movie night. You love movie night because you get to use your popcorn popper and make freshly popped popcorn for the family. You notice that your usual brand of corn kernels is on sale for $2.55 for a large bag (enough for 5 family movie nights). You want to take advantage of this sale and grab 2 bags. You have a coupon for $0.80 off of 2 bags. How much do you pay for both bags of popcorn kernels?

Keep going...

2) Just last week, your family was running low on toothpaste, so you purchased a new tube and used a half off coupon. This week however, you see that there is a coupon stuck on the side of your normal brand. Not only is this toothpaste on clearance for half-off its normal price, but the coupon stuck on the box is for an additional $0.45 off. If your brand normally costs $4.50, what is the cost of the toothpaste today?

3) Your mother loves a whole grain cereal that has dried cranberries and walnuts. She eats her cereal every morning and you planned to buy one box for her breakfast for the week. You notice that there is an in-store coupon hanging next to your mother's favorite cereal brand. The coupon offers 1 free box when you purchase 2. Each box normally costs $3.77. How much are you saving but taking advantage of this deal instead of purchasing 3 separate boxes of cereal?

A few more in-store scenerios...

4) Once a week, after gymnastics class, your friend Molly comes over for a play date. You both love to make spinach quesadillas together. You have everything that you need at home except for the frozen spinach. You only planned to get 2 large bags of frozen spinach at $1.33 each for the week. However, there is an in-store coupon for 6 bags of frozen spinach for $6. How much do you save but taking advantage of the 6-bag sale?

5) Your father makes delicious vegetable lasagna. Three times a year, he makes 4 large batches of lasagna and places them in the freezer to eat at a later date. In order to make 4 batches of his dish, he needs one bottle of dried basil and one bottle of oregano from the spice aisle. Your father's brand of spices has an in-store coupon that is good for 2 spices for $5 instead of $4.70 each. Dried herbs last for up to 3 years. You decide to buy $15 worth. How much do would 6 bottles cost if you don't take advantage of this deal?

6) Toilet paper is always a great item to stock up on. You usually buy the large package of your favorite brand at $9.60 for 20 rolls. However there is an in-store sale on the smaller packs of 4 rolls for $1.05. There is a 10-pack limit. You decide to take advantage of this deal. How much money are you saving by purchasing 10 smaller packs then 2 larger 20 roll packs?

7) You love to cook and your parents allow you to make new recipes for the family to try. Your delicious tuna casserole with extra vegetables was not on the menu for this week, but it may be on the menu soon as you spot a great in-store coupon for cans of tuna. Each can is normally $0.84 each but the sale is for 3 cans for $1.50. You need 6 cans for your casserole. How much would six cans cost if they were not on sale? How much will six cans cost at the sales price?

More in-store scenerios...

8) Your family makes many healthy meals throughout the week with brown rice. This week, your mother is making a delicious meal of salmon and roasted vegetables to go with the brown rice. You only need a small bag of brown rice ($2.11 each) for the dish but you notice that the larger bag (the size of 2 bags) is only $3.45. How much are you saving but purchasing one larger bag instead of 2 smaller bags? How much are you saving by purchasing 3 larger bags?

9) You love to make hot chocolate with vanilla almond milk. One box of almond milk is usually $2.19. There is an in-store coupon for $0.75 off each box if you buy five boxes. How much are you saving by purchasing 5 boxes on sale?

10) You have enough shampoo to last you for another two weeks but you see that your favorite berry scented shampoo is not only half-off but there is an in-store coupon for an additional $0.35 off. The original price is $5. You decide to purchase 2 bottles to take advantage of this amazing deal. How much is the cost of both bottles?

11) Every Sunday during football season, your parents invite their friends over to watch a game. You love to make your famous turkey chili. You have everything that you need for the batch that you are making for this coming Sunday but notice that cans of kidney beans are on sale for $0.92 a can (regularly $1.40). You can purchase up to ten cans of kidney beans with this sale. Your recipe calls for 2 cans per batch of chili. How many batches of chili will 10 cans allow you to make? How much are you saving by purchasing the 10 cans on sale?

Multiplication

Multiplication is the best and quickest way to add up in-store savings. Multiplication is repeated addition and is the quickest way to add grocery totals or potential savings. Knowing your multiplication is key to being a Chief Couponing Officer. Try the following problems.

ex. 5+5+5+5= 5x4=   20

1)   4+4+4+4+4   =   =

2)   2+2+2   =   =

3)   7+7+7+7   =   =

4)   9+9   =   =

5)   10+10+10   =   =

6)   6+6+6+6+6   =   =

7)   11+11+11+11   =   =

8)   13+13+13+13   =   =

9)   5+5+5   =   =

10)   20+20+20   =   =

11)   1+1+1+1+1+1   =   =

12)   17+17+17   =   =

13)   22+22   =   =

14)   19+19+19+19   =   =

15)   50+50   =   =

16)   33+33+33+33   =   =

17)   100+100   =   =

18)   8+8+8+8+8+8   =   =

19)   5+5+5+5+5+5   =   =

Now try the reverse... ex. 20= 5x4= 5+5+5+5

20)   40   =   5   x   =

21)   50   =   10   x   =

22)   90   =   9   x   =

23)   70   =   7   x   =

24)   20   =   4   x   =

25)   25   =   5   x   =

26)   22   =   11   x   =

27)   30   =   10   x   =

28)   45   =   9   x   =

29)   21   =   7   x   =

30)   44   =   11   x   =

Multiplying Money

Sample ➝

      1 1
1) $1.55
   x   3
   ———
   $4.65

Sample ➝

1) $3.45
  x   2
  ———

1) $6.25
  x 2

2) $7.85
  x 4

3) $9.22
  x 3

4) $3.43
  x 5

5) $5.78
  x 9

6) $4.93
  x 8

7) $3.18
  x 6

8) $2.17
  x 3

9) $5.92
  x 4

10) $2.36
  x 7

11) $9.18
  x 2

12) $6.67
  x 8

13) $8.35
  x 6

14) $9.53
  x 3

15) $5.02
  x 9

16) $4.18
  x 7

17) $7.23
  x 6

18) $9.53
  x 3

19) $5.02
  x 9

20) $4.18
  x 7

21) $7.23
  x 6

22) $8.36 x 5	23) $2.11 x 5	24) $9.12 x 2	25) $2.56 x 9
26) $4.43 x 9	27) $7.31 x 7	28) $5.26 x 2	29) $9.44 x 5
30) $2.28 x 3	31) $17.55 x 2	32) $16.67 x 3	33) $19.94 x 6
34) $12.68 x 5	35) $23.64 x 6	36) $60.12 x 3	37) $18.77 x 2
38) $38.99 x 5	39) $19.19 x 7	40) $22.24 x 9	41) $44.44 x 9
42) $42.78 x 4	43) $66.33 x 2	44) $80.12 x 8	45) $14.13 x 6
46) $19.44 x 3	47) $41.40 x 5	48) $52.25 x 8	49) $25.78 x 4

50) $14.16 x 9	51) $62.91 x 5	52) $79.33 x 3	53) $72.26 x 2
54) $70.09 x 8	55) $33.31 x 4	56) $55.55 x 7	57) $49.84 x 6
58) $76.11 x 8	59) $32.11 x 2	60) $22.77 x 8	61) $74.31 x 4
62) $12.12 x 9	63) $46.64 x 7	64) $46.80 x 3	65) $16.76 x 5
66) $33.33 x 5	67) $11.61 x 4	68) $89.90 x 3	69) $17.70 x 9
70) $72.68 x 6	71) $90.43 x 3	72) $56.19 x 8	73) $74.33 x 8
74) $23.74 x 2	75) $71.60 x 5	76) $98.11 x 7	77) $44.90 x 3

78) $75.06
x   8

79) $82.15
x   5

80) $81.12
x   4

81) $52.46
x   2

82) $34.21
x   9

83) $77.80
x   6

84) $65.96
x   8

85) $29.43
x   8

86) $32.21
x   3

87) $55.62
x   2

88) $49.90
x   1

89) $69.22
x   5

90) $28.82
x   6

91) $33.60
x   9

92) $64.46
x   2

93) $88.27
x   5

94) $44.99
x   3

95) $35.19
x   7

96) $92.54
x   8

97) $51.25
x   6

98) $71.17
x   4

99) $36.53
x   5

100) $88.34
x   2

101) $39.98
x   3

Keep Multiplying...

Keep going! Make sure that you double check your work and add dollar signs and decimals to your answers.

1) $15.57
   x   7
   _____

2) $17.76
   x   2
   _____

3) $32.71
   x   6
   _____

4) $48.33
   x   9
   _____

5) $26.97
   x   7
   _____

6) $74.52
   x   8
   _____

7) $25.37
   x   5
   _____

8) $53.62
   x   7
   _____

9) $40.15
   x   4
   _____

10) $27.25
    x   5
    _____

11) $64.77
    x   2
    _____

12) $11.29
    x   6
    _____

13) $32.73
    x   2
    _____

14) $15.63
    x   2
    _____

15) $80.39
    x   4
    _____

16) $32.90
    x   7
    _____

17) $29.99
    x   5
    _____

18) $39.01
    x   8
    _____

19) $55.92
    x   6
    _____

20) $19.80
    x   3
    _____

21) $44.77
    x   5
    _____

22) $72.28
    x   5
    _____

23) $95.04
    x   9
    _____

24) $10.07
    x   7
    _____

25) $67.13
    x   2
    _____

More Multiplication...

26) $91.16
x   3

27) $32.90
x   2

28) $18.28
x   9

29) $79.90
x   8

30) $28.53
x   6

31) $66.99
x   4

32) $27.11
x   6

33) $41.08
x   5

34) $41.98
x   7

35) $11.67
x   9

36) $86.00
x   3

37) $71.22
x   5

38) $11.19
x   4

39) $99.44
x   6

40) $84.72
x   8

41) $59.02
x   2

42) $30.96
x   5

43) $38.20
x   6

44) $72.79
x   7

45) $89.27
x   3

46) $33.29
x   8

47) $91.24
x   2

48) $77.22
x   3

49) $83.83
x   9

Multiplication Word Problems

1) You need 16 apples for pies that you are preparing for your schools bake sale. Each apple costs $0.47 each. How much are the apples?

2) You need to bring a snack to a sleepover. You decide that you will bring granola bars. Each bar is $1.27. You, plus 6 of your friends, will need a granola bar. How much will the granola bars costs?

3) Your birthday party is on Saturday and you need party hats for all 17 of your guests. Each hat costs $0.98 each. How much will your party hats costs?

More Multiplication...

4) You are bringing oranges to your soccer game. You purchase 26 oranges at $0.39 a piece. How much did you spend on oranges?

5) There are ears of corn on sale for $0.58 each. You need 12 ears of corn to make chowder. How much will your ears of corn cost?

6) Salmon fillets are $8.83 each. You will use 2 for dinner and purchase 3 to place in the freezer for a later date. How much will your salmon fillets cost?

7) Your family needs 3 loaves of bread for sandwiches for lunch. Each loaf of bread is $3.82. How much will you spend on bread?

8) Your father's shaving cream is on sale for $2.77 per can. There is a limit of 8 cans and you want to take advantage of this deal. How much will all 8 cans of shaving cream cost?

9) You need 2 jars of peanut butter for the week and they are on sale for $2.68 each. You are limited to purchasing 10 jars and want to take advantage of the sale. How much will 10 jars of peanut butter cost?

Take a Trial Run!

It is really important to have an idea of what your grocery total will be and how much you will possibly save with coupons especially if you are on a weekly budget. Practice makes perfect so let's try adding up the following purchases, subtract your coupon savings and estimate your total bill. Take a quick look at the list first and try your best to add up the total in your head. Write this "guess" or estimation on the estimation line. Then use the open space to calculate the actual answer. Write the actual total below.

Trial Run Week #1

grapes	2 lbs.	$2.33 per lb.
oranges	3 lbs.	$1.75 per lb.
5 avocados		$0.77 each
1 loaf of bread		$2.67 ($0.20 off coupon)
butter (1 container)		$1.56 ($0.45 off coupon)

Estimation $_____

Actual Total:_____

Trial Run Week #2

bananas 4lbs.	$0.99 per lb.
2 jars of peanut butter	$3.99 each
4 bags of fresh spinach	$1.39 each
2 blocks of cheddar cheese	$3.40 each
1 pack of flour tortillas	$2.65 ($0.75 off coupon)

Estimation $_____

Actual Total:_____

Trial Run Week #3

8 mangoes	$0.99 each
2 pineapples	$1.35 each
3 papayas	$2.55 each
2 bags of kale	$2.50 each ($0.50 coupon off each bag)
1 gallon of skim milk	$4.05
1 bag of chia seeds	$3.90
1 box of corn flakes	$4.20 ($0.60 off coupon)
1 gallon of orange juice	$2.90
2 bags of veggie chips	$3.33 each
1 pack of dental floss	$4.11
1 bottle of mouthwash	$6.75 ($1 off coupon)

Estimation $_____

Actual Total:_____

Trial Run Week #4

2 bottles of olive oil	$7.99 each
5 tomatoes	$0.45 each
1 lb. of fresh basil	$3.25
1 container of sea salt	$2.11
1 jar of black olives	$4.49
2 bottles of balsamic vinegar	$3.76 each
2 bags of spaghetti noodles	$1.80 each (1 $0.25 off coupon)
3 bottles of marinara sauce	$2.05 each
1 jar of crushed garlic	$3.88
2 packs of ground turkey	$5.90 each

Estimation $_____

Actual Total:_____

Trial Run Week #5

1 large bag of brown rice	$4.15
2 lbs. of zucchini	$0.75 each
2 red bell peppers	$0.40 each
2 green bell pepper	$0.42 each
mushrooms 2lbs.	$2.55 each lb.
3 large carrots	$1.90 total
5 cans of tuna	$1.24 each (2 $0.50 off coupons)
2 bags of frozen peas	$2.30
1 bag of frozen corn	$2.60
2 cans of of lentil soup	$0.98 each
7 cans of cat food	$1.40 each (7 $0.15 off coupons)

Estimation $_____

Actual Total:_____

Divide Your Savings by 3

The money that you save as a Chief Couponing Officer should be divided into three parts:

Part 1: Personal savings

Every person needs a "rainy day" savings. This money is to be placed in a savings account and not touched unless absolutely necessary. This is not the money that you spend on fun items every week. However, this is the money that you hold on to and watch grow with interest from the bank and your weekly deposits.

Part 2: Spending Money

It takes a lot of wonderful hard work to be a successful Chief Couponing Officer and you deserve a treat or two for your effort. With your parent's permission, decide on a item that you would like to buy such as a magazine, new music or tickets to a movie. You may even consider not buying smaller items and saving your spending money for a bigger item at a later date.

Part 3: Investments

There are many ways that you can invest money but the best way to invest the coupon savings should be to purchase items that will help your family for a long period of time. The ideal method of investing for your family is to start a garden! A sure way to cut down on spending money at the grocery store is to grow your own herbs, fruit and vegetables. Organic seeds, soil, gardening tools and fruit trees should be purchased with a portion of the savings.

Let's try a few problems...

1) You love to make lemonade. Five years ago, your mother purchased a lemon tree for $33. The tree is now beautiful and full of large lemons that you can pick all year long. You need 8 lemons to make one pitcher of lemonade. At the grocery store, each lemon is $0.77. How much would it cost to make 5 pitchers of lemonade with store bought lemons?

2) A pack of seeds for salad greens costs $1.22. You planted the seeds in the window box outside of your kitchen window and now you have enough salad greens to make a large salad for your family to go with 4 dinners! A large bag of salad greens at the store cost $4.67. How much would it cost if you had to purchase the salad greens for 4 salads at the grocery store?

Keep going...

3) Guacamole and pita chips are one of your family's favorite snacks. A few years ago, your father purchased an avocado tree and it now produces so many avocados that you share them with your neighbors. To make 1 delicious bowl of guacamole, you need five ripe avocados. Avocados can cost up to $2.58 a piece at the store! How much would it cost to make 3 bowls of guacamole with store bought avocados?

4) Your family eats many tomatoes throughout the week in sauces, soups, salads and even alone as snacks. You purchased hanging tomato planters that produce so many tomatoes that you never have to purchase any from the grocery store. For dinner your family used 16 cherry tomatoes in a salad and 11 Roma tomatoes for marinara sauce. At the grocery store, cherry tomatoes are $0.66 for 2 and Roma tomatoes are $0.65 each. How much would your dinner cost if you had to purchase your tomatoes in the grocery store?

A few more...

5) You love to drink strawberry and banana smoothies for breakfast. Each smoothie needs 10 strawberries. You are able to go to your garden every morning and pick fresh strawberries to use. A basket of 10 strawberries costs $5.88 at the store. How much would strawberries for a smoothie every day for 10 days cost if you purchased them from the store?

6) Your family has an amazing herb garden filled with basil, cilantro, parsley, oregano, dill and mint. Your mother uses the fresh mint in her tea. Your mint plant produces enough mint for 5 cups of tea every week. One box of mint tea with five tea bags at the store costs $3.99. How much would it cost for your mother to make 25 cups of tea if you had to purchase the tea from the grocery store?

Savings Log

Use this Savings Log to track the money that you save using coupons over a 12-month period. At the end of the year, total up the entire amount that you saved your family being a Chief Couponing Officer.

$$$$$$

Date:_____

Total price of groceries:_____

Coupon savings:_____

Percentage of savings:_____

$$$$$$

Date:_____

Total price of groceries:_____

Coupon savings:_____

Percentage of savings:_____

$$$$$$

Date:_____

Total price of groceries:_____

Coupon savings:_____

Percentage of savings:_____

$$$$$$

Date:_____

Total price of groceries:_____

Coupon savings:_____

Percentage of savings:_____

$$$$$$

Date:_____

Total price of groceries:_____

Coupon savings:_____

Percentage of savings:_____

$$$$$$

Date:_____

Total price of groceries:_____

Coupon savings:_____

Percentage of savings:_____

For additional savings log sheets, visit www.SorinaFant.com

$$$$$$

Date:_____

Total price of groceries:_____

Coupon savings:_____

Percentage of savings:_____

$$$$$$

Date:_____

Total price of groceries:_____

Coupon savings:_____

Percentage of savings:_____

$$$$$$

Date:_____

Total price of groceries:_____

Coupon savings:_____

Percentage of savings:_____

$$$$$$

Date:_____

Total price of groceries:_____

Coupon savings:_____

Percentage of savings:_____

$$$$$$

Date:_____

Total price of groceries:_____

Coupon savings:_____

Percentage of savings:_____

$$$$$$

Date:_____

Total price of groceries:_____

Coupon savings:_____

Percentage of savings:_____

$$$$$$

Date:_____

Total price of groceries:_____

Coupon savings:_____

Percentage of savings:_____

$$$$$$

Date:_____

Total price of groceries:_____

Coupon savings:_____

Percentage of savings:_____

$$$$$$

Date:_____

Total price of groceries:_____

Coupon savings:_____

Percentage of savings:_____

$$$$$$

Date:_____

Total price of groceries:_____

Coupon savings:_____

Percentage of savings:_____

$$$$$$

Date:_____

Total price of groceries:_____

Coupon savings:_____

Percentage of savings:_____

$$$$$$

Date:_____

Total price of groceries:_____

Coupon savings:_____

Percentage of savings:_____

$$$$$$

Date:_____

Total price of groceries:_____

Coupon savings:_____

Percentage of savings:_____

$$$$$$

Date:_____

Total price of groceries:_____

Coupon savings:_____

Percentage of savings:_____

$$$$$$

Date:_____

Total price of groceries:_____

Coupon savings:_____

Percentage of savings:_____

$$$$$$

Date:_____

Total price of groceries:_____

Coupon savings:_____

Percentage of savings:_____

$$$$$$

Date:_____

Total price of groceries:_____

Coupon savings:_____

Percentage of savings:_____

$$$$$$

Date:_____

Total price of groceries:_____

Coupon savings:_____

Percentage of savings:_____

$$$$$$

Date:_____

Total price of groceries:_____

Coupon savings:_____

Percentage of savings:_____

$$$$$$

Date:_____

Total price of groceries:_____

Coupon savings:_____

Percentage of savings:_____

$$$$$$

Date:_____

Total price of groceries:_____

Coupon savings:_____

Percentage of savings:_____

$$$$$$

Date:_____

Total price of groceries:_____

Coupon savings:_____

Percentage of savings:_____

$$$$$$

Date:_____

Total price of groceries:_____

Coupon savings:_____

Percentage of savings:_____

$$$$$$

Date:_____

Total price of groceries:_____

Coupon savings:_____

Percentage of savings:_____

$$$$$$

Date:_____

Total price of groceries:_____

Coupon savings:_____

Percentage of savings:_____

$$$$$$

Date:_____

Total price of groceries:_____

Coupon savings:_____

Percentage of savings:_____

$$$$$$

Date:_____

Total price of groceries:_____

Coupon savings:_____

Percentage of savings:_____

$$$$$$

Date:_____

Total price of groceries:_____

Coupon savings:_____

Percentage of savings:_____

$$$$$$

Date:_____

Total price of groceries:_____

Coupon savings:_____

Percentage of savings:_____

$$$$$$

Date:_____

Total price of groceries:_____

Coupon savings:_____

Percentage of savings:_____

$$$$$$

Date:_____

Total price of groceries:_____

Coupon savings:_____

Percentage of savings:_____

$$$$$$

Date:_____

Total price of groceries:_____

Coupon savings:_____

Percentage of savings:_____

$$$$$$

Date:_____

Total price of groceries:_____

Coupon savings:_____

Percentage of savings:_____

$$$$$$

Date:_____

Total price of groceries:_____

Coupon savings:_____

Percentage of savings:_____

$$$$$$

Date:_____

Total price of groceries:_____

Coupon savings:_____

Percentage of savings:_____

For additional savings log sheets, visit www.SorinaFant.com

$$$$$$

Date:_____

Total price of groceries:_____

Coupon savings:_____

Percentage of savings:_____

$$$$$$

Date:_____

Total price of groceries:_____

Coupon savings:_____

Percentage of savings:_____

$$$$$$

Date:_____

Total price of groceries:_____

Coupon savings:_____

Percentage of savings:_____

$$$$$$

Date:_____

Total price of groceries:_____

Coupon savings:_____

Percentage of savings:_____

$$$$$$

Date:_____

Total price of groceries:_____

Coupon savings:_____

Percentage of savings:_____

$$$$$$

Date:_____

Total price of groceries:_____

Coupon savings:_____

Percentage of savings:_____

$$$$$$

Date:_____

Total price of groceries:_____

Coupon savings:_____

Percentage of savings:_____

$$$$$$

Date:_____

Total price of groceries:_____

Coupon savings:_____

Percentage of savings:_____

$$$$$$

Date:_____

Total price of groceries:_____

Coupon savings:_____

Percentage of savings:_____

$$$$$$

Date:_____

Total price of groceries:_____

Coupon savings:_____

Percentage of savings:_____

$$$$$$

Date:_____

Total price of groceries:_____

Coupon savings:_____

Percentage of savings:_____

$$$$$$

Date:_____

Total price of groceries:_____

Coupon savings:_____

Percentage of savings:_____

$$$$$$

Date:_____

Total price of groceries:_____

Coupon savings:_____

Percentage of savings:_____

$$$$$$

Date:_____

Total price of groceries:_____

Coupon savings:_____

Percentage of savings:_____

$$$$$$

Date:_____

Total price of groceries:_____

Coupon savings:_____

Percentage of savings:_____

$$$$$$

Date:_____

Total price of groceries:_____

Coupon savings:_____

Percentage of savings:_____

$$$$$$

Date:_____

Total price of groceries:_____

Coupon savings:_____

Percentage of savings:_____

$$$$$$

Date:_____

Total price of groceries:_____

Coupon savings:_____

Percentage of savings:_____

$$$$$$

Date:_____

Total price of groceries:_____

Coupon savings:_____

Percentage of savings:_____

$$$$$$

Date:_____

Total price of groceries:_____

Coupon savings:_____

Percentage of savings:_____

$$$$$$

Date:_____

Total price of groceries:_____

Coupon savings:_____

Percentage of savings:_____

$$$$$$

Date:_____

Total price of groceries:_____

Coupon savings:_____

Percentage of savings:_____

$$$$$$

Date:_____

Total price of groceries:_____

Coupon savings:_____

Percentage of savings:_____

$$$$$$

Date:_____

Total price of groceries:_____

Coupon savings:_____

Percentage of savings:_____

$$$$$$

Date:_____

Total price of groceries:_____

Coupon savings:_____

Percentage of savings:_____

$$$$$$

Date:_____

Total price of groceries:_____

Coupon savings:_____

Percentage of savings:_____

$$$$$$

Date:_____

Total price of groceries:_____

Coupon savings:_____

Percentage of savings:_____

$$$$$$

Date:_____

Total price of groceries:_____

Coupon savings:_____

Percentage of savings:_____

$$$$$$

Date:_____

Total price of groceries:_____

Coupon savings:_____

Percentage of savings:_____

$$$$$$

Date:_____

Total price of groceries:_____

Coupon savings:_____

Percentage of savings:_____

$$$$$$

Date:_____

Total price of groceries:_____

Coupon savings:_____

Percentage of savings:_____

$$$$$$

Date:_____

Total price of groceries:_____

Coupon savings:_____

Percentage of savings:_____

$$$$$$

Date:_____

Total price of groceries:_____

Coupon savings:_____

Percentage of savings:_____

$$$$$$

Date:_____

Total price of groceries:_____

Coupon savings:_____

Percentage of savings:_____

$$$$$$

Date:_____

Total price of groceries:_____

Coupon savings:_____

Percentage of savings:_____

How Much Did You Save This Year?

Calculate the amount of money that you have saved your family this year.

Total: _____

CONGRATULATIONS!
You are an official
Chief Couponing Officer!

What's Next? Become a Personal Shopper!

The best thing that you can do after mastering a new skill is to invest time into turning that new skill into a profitable business. Become a CEO, or Chief Executive Officer, and turn your skills as a Chief Couponing Officer into a successful business! With your parent's permission, ask family members, friends and neighbors if you can be their Chief Couponing Officer and help them to save money on their grocery bill. Speak with your parents and come up with a percentage of the money that you save your clients to act as your compensation. Visit www.SorinaFant.com to purchase the CEO workbook that will help you to set up a successful business.

Here are a few business cards to get you started:

Chief Couponing Officer

✂----------

_____
(Name)

I can help you save money on your grocery bill!

_____
(Number and email)

Chief Couponing Officer

✂----------

_____
(Name)

I can help you save money on your grocery bill!

_____
(Number and email)

---

www.ingramcontent.com/pod-product-compliance
Lightning Source LLC
Chambersburg PA
CBHW081151040426
42445CB00015B/1841